FIRE AND OTHER FEELINGS

BY

AMBIVALENTLY
yours

THOUGHT
CATALOG
Books

THOUGHTCATALOG.COM
NEW YORK · LOS ANGELES

THOUGHT CATALOG Books

Published by Thought Catalog Books, an imprint of the digital magazine Thought Catalog, which is owned and operated by The Thought & Expression Company LLC, an independent media organization based in Brooklyn, New York and Los Angeles, California.

This book was produced by Chris Lavergne and Noelle Beams. Special thanks to KJ Parish for print art direction and Isidoros Karamitopoulos for circulation management.

thoughtcatalog.com | shopcatalog.com

Made in the United States of America.

ISBN 978-1-949759-55-6

(drawings, poems & stories)

FIRE

1

There is a small town somewhere in the United States that has been on fire for 60 years. The fire was set intentionally and innocently to clear a landfill, but unexpectedly took possession of a network of abandoned coal mines that slept under the entire town. What started as a controlled burn got so out of hand that to this day, no one has been able to put the fire out. The flames are not flamboyantly present, they mostly live in the dark, under splitting roads and small houses habitually filling with toxic gas. When it was understood that the fire was too stubborn to be tamed, authorities gave up their firefighting and decided to relocate all of the town's residents instead. A few inhabitants stayed behind, committing to living a life on fire, because even in a ramshackle state the town was still their home. I'm not sure if their resolution is bravery or recklessness, but as someone who is on fire herself, all I can think is, "I know how you feel."

I can't remember when my fire started. Maybe I was on fire before my memory learned how to hold onto things. Maybe the fire crept in so slowly, I just didn't notice it.

When I say "on fire" I don't use the word "fire" as a metaphor for passion or rage, or any other dramatic emotion that fire is asked to carry. For me it is all very literal: sometimes I just catch fire.

The fire doesn't cause me tangible pain or leave visible marks. The flames are tempered to my body heat, they slip through my skin like thieves, quick and greedy. They are a physical reaction that takes and breaks, reveals, and recedes, like tides but hotter. I think the fire is tethered to something inside of me that I can't quite touch, something that wants to assert itself. It excavates without permission, I witness it without will.

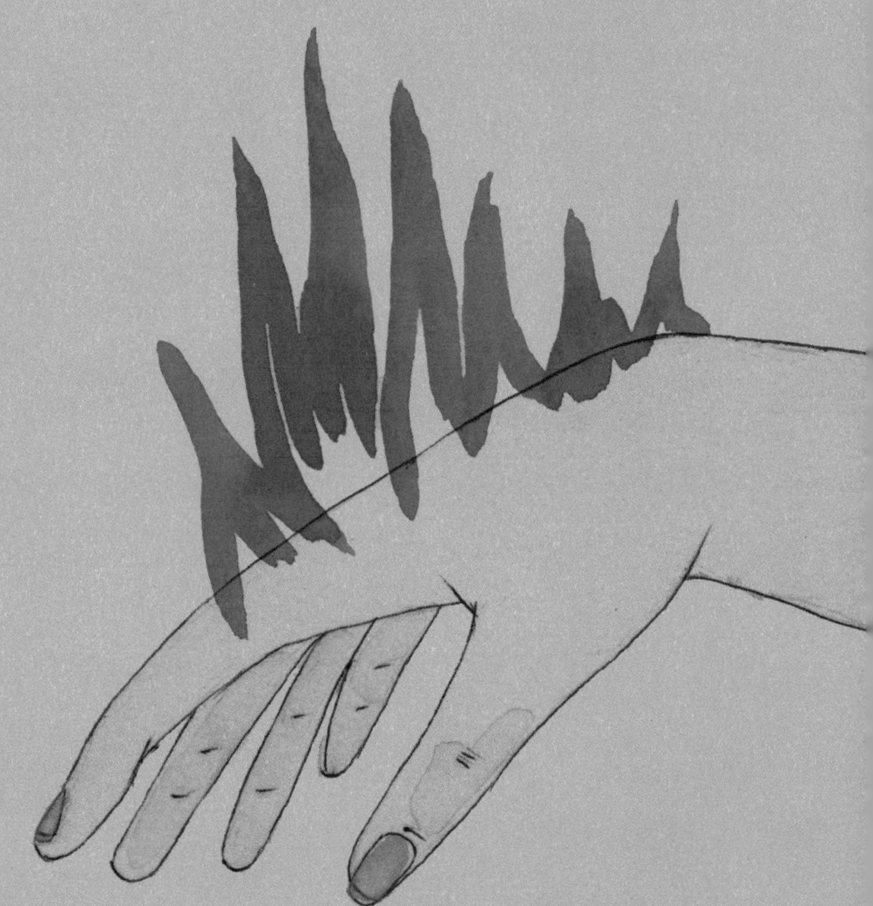

I never know where the flames will appear but I can always feel them coming. They start as a warm tingle in my hands or a scratch at the back of my throat, then the heat dances on the edge of my skin until the flames choose a place to manifest. Sometimes my arms catch fire, other times my legs, or my back, or my neck, or my stomach, or my face. The worst is when the flames settle on my face.

It's hard to act like everything is fine with fire in your eyes.

I'm at my best
Teary eyed
And fuzzy socked

The floral armour
You always mistook
For weakness

WHEN I WAS ANGRY
YOU TOLD ME
TO BE SOFT

WHEN I WAS SOFT
YOU TOLD ME
TO BE STRONG

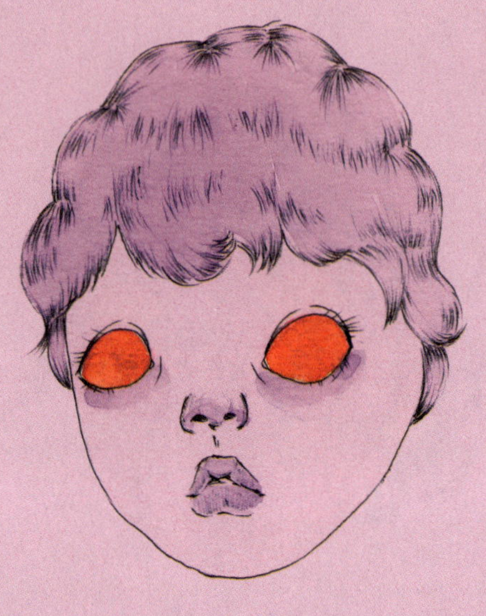

WHEN I WAS STRONG
YOU TOLD ME
TO BE QUIET

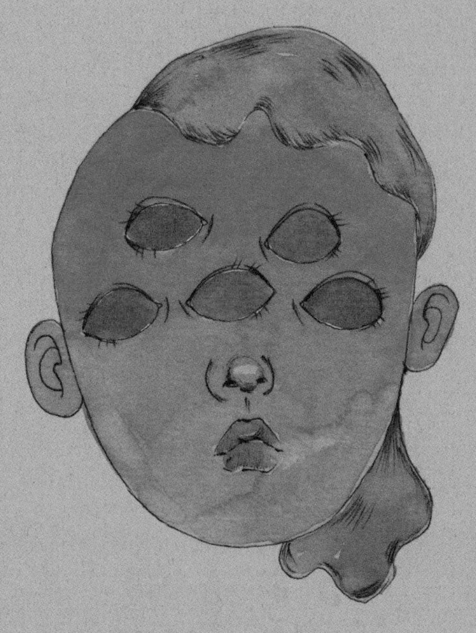

WHEN I WAS QUIET
IT ALWAYS
MADE ME ANGRY

I LIKE TO COAT
MY TENDER
FEELINGS
WITH RAGE
A PRICKLY
EXTERIOR
TO HOLD MY
SOFT CENTER

WHAT YOU SEE
IS RARELY
WHAT YOU GET

I LIKE TO
DO THINGS
THE HARD
WAY

SO I CAN
TELL MYSELF
THAT NO
OUTWARD
CHALLENGE
WILL EVER
BE WORSE

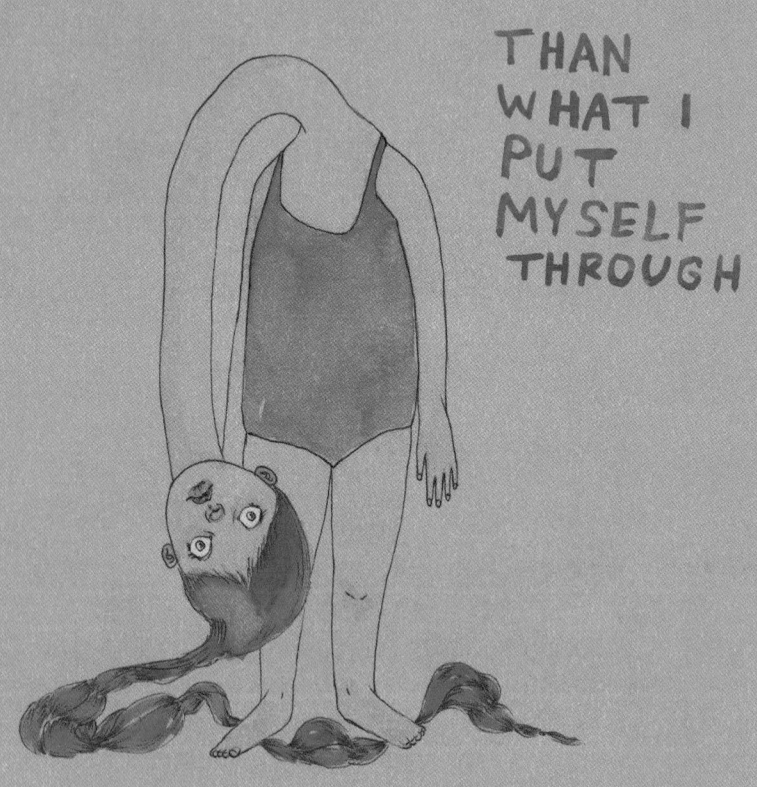
THAN
WHAT I
PUT
MYSELF
THROUGH

*SPOILER ALERT:

I DO NOT
RECOMMEND

WATER

2

I always try to hide the fire, or at least to water it down a little. I soak my body in cold water before I leave the house, convinced that if my skin is sufficiently waterlogged it will not be able to hold a flame. My efforts are always a little futile, but the act of it, the ritual soak, has become a crucial part of my day. I've scared myself into thinking that if I don't drown my skin a little, the fire will take hold of me in a way I have not dared to think of yet.

The water never stays on my skin though. It sinks in, then comes out of my eyes, my armpits, and my upper lip as tears and sweat, betraying everything I try to hold tight. Instead of a calm sea, I'm just a waterfall on fire.

A few people close to me have caught me arms deep in the kitchen sink, soaking my skin diligently. They never say anything but I can feel them collecting these moments and adding them to their memorized idea of me. I catch the discomfort it brings them to see the cracks in my armour so exposed. I'm getting better at hiding it. Not just the fire, but the lengths I go to to hide the fire. I hide the flames by hiding parts of who I am, by missing out on things or getting there late, by letting them think I am a little uncaring, a little aloof, rather than a little on fire. Shame is such a lonely feeling.

The worst is when people see the flames. Worse yet is when people feel inclined to help. Some approach me unsolicitedly with a fire extinguisher or a thick blanket and try to suffocate the flames right off of me. They don't understand that my fire is not like a kitchen fire that catches by mistake and needs to be put out as urgently as possible. My fire is stubborn and has deep roots. Where it burns is not where it began. Applying pressure to its place of manifestation just entices it to appear elsewhere.

Other people get annoyed with me when they catch me burning too often. "Just put it out!" they say, as though burning alive is an intentional act that I can just think my way out of. And of course, when all else fails then come the suggestions of yoga routines, vegan/gluten/dairy-free diets, meditation, and the odd crystal combination. All of these suggestions are paired with anecdotal evidence, and my inability to tame my fire with the same efficacy as strangers is seen as a failure of my character.

And of course, the more I fail, the more I burn.

I want to feel things
Without excess
To be filled
But not consumed
Not cool
Not tepid
Full feelings
Half the mess

Maybe it's because
The moon is in Scorpio
Or maybe I don't
Understand
Astrology
At all
But I want to release
Everything
All my fears
All my dreams
All my expectations
I want to
Marie Kondo
My emotional history
Find sparks of joy
In absence
I want to feel
Everything
From nothing
Nonetheless
I know
I'm too
Sentimental
To sort
The necessary
From the excess

I HIDE MY
EMOTIONS
ALL OVER
MY BODY

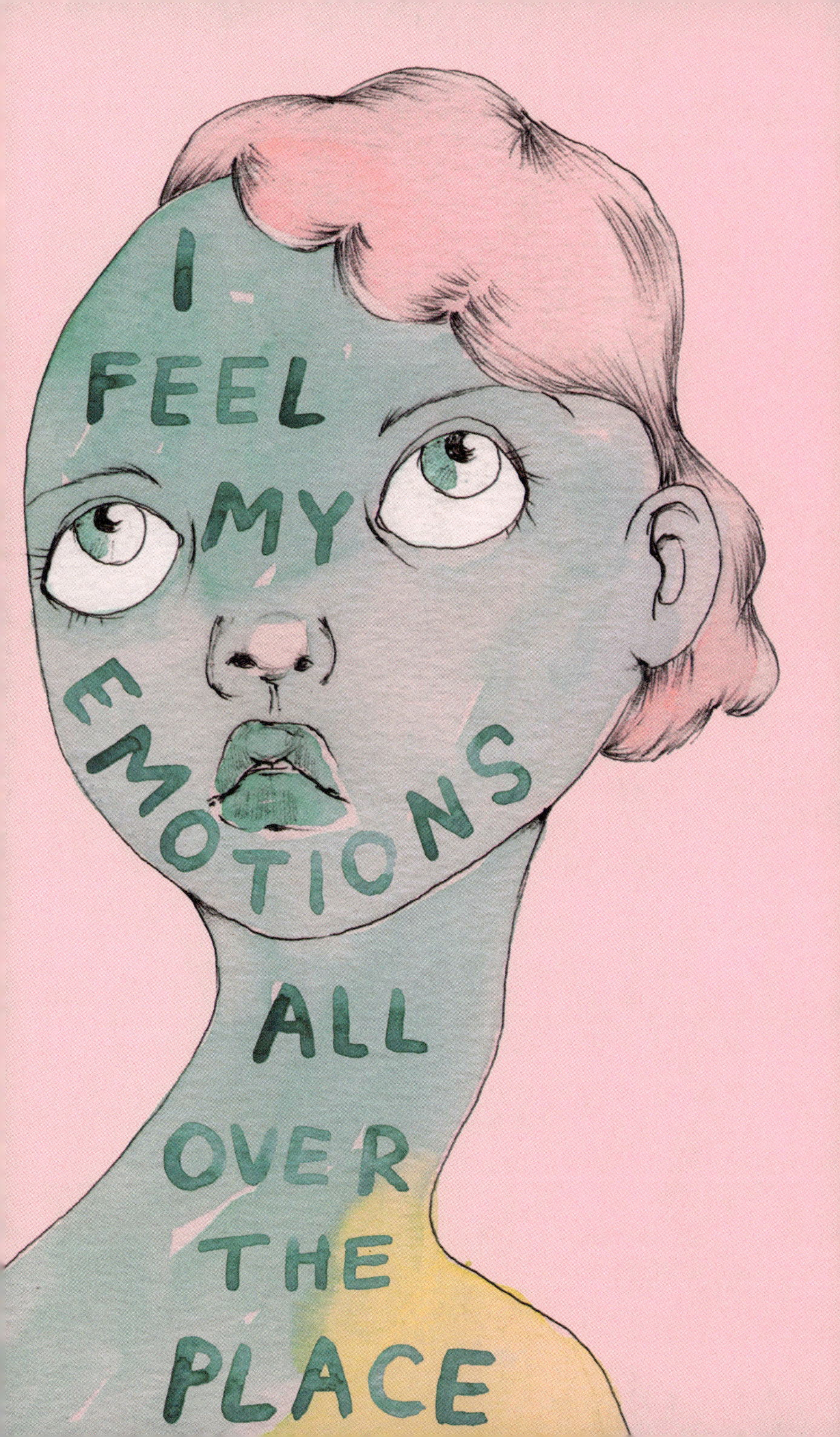
I
FEEL
MY
EMOTIONS
ALL
OVER
THE
PLACE

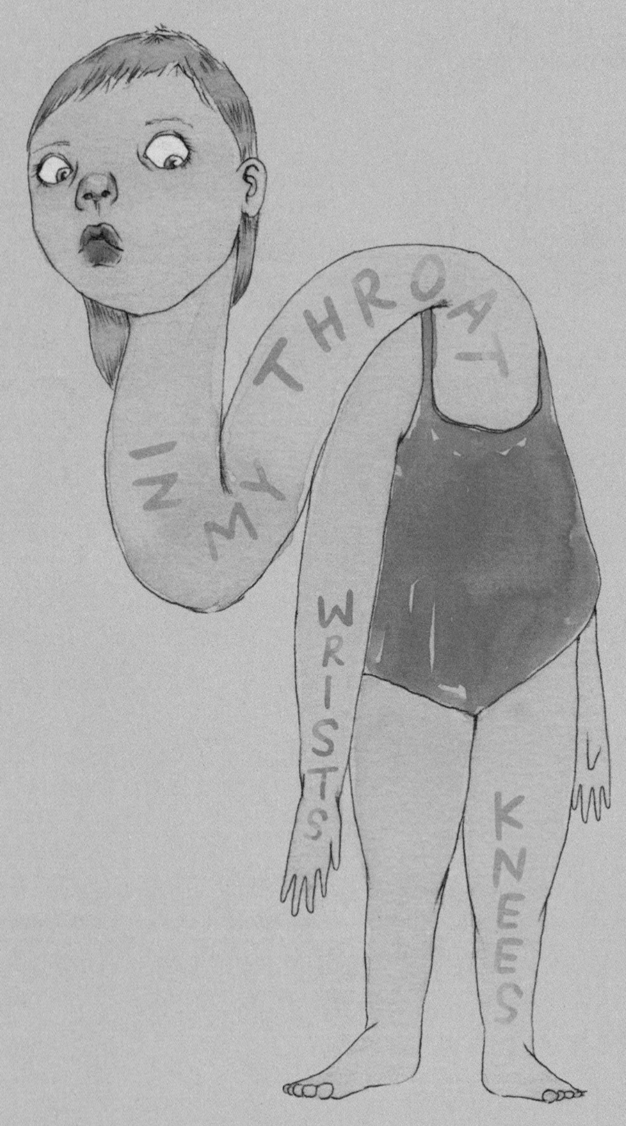
IN MY THROAT
WRISTS
KNEES

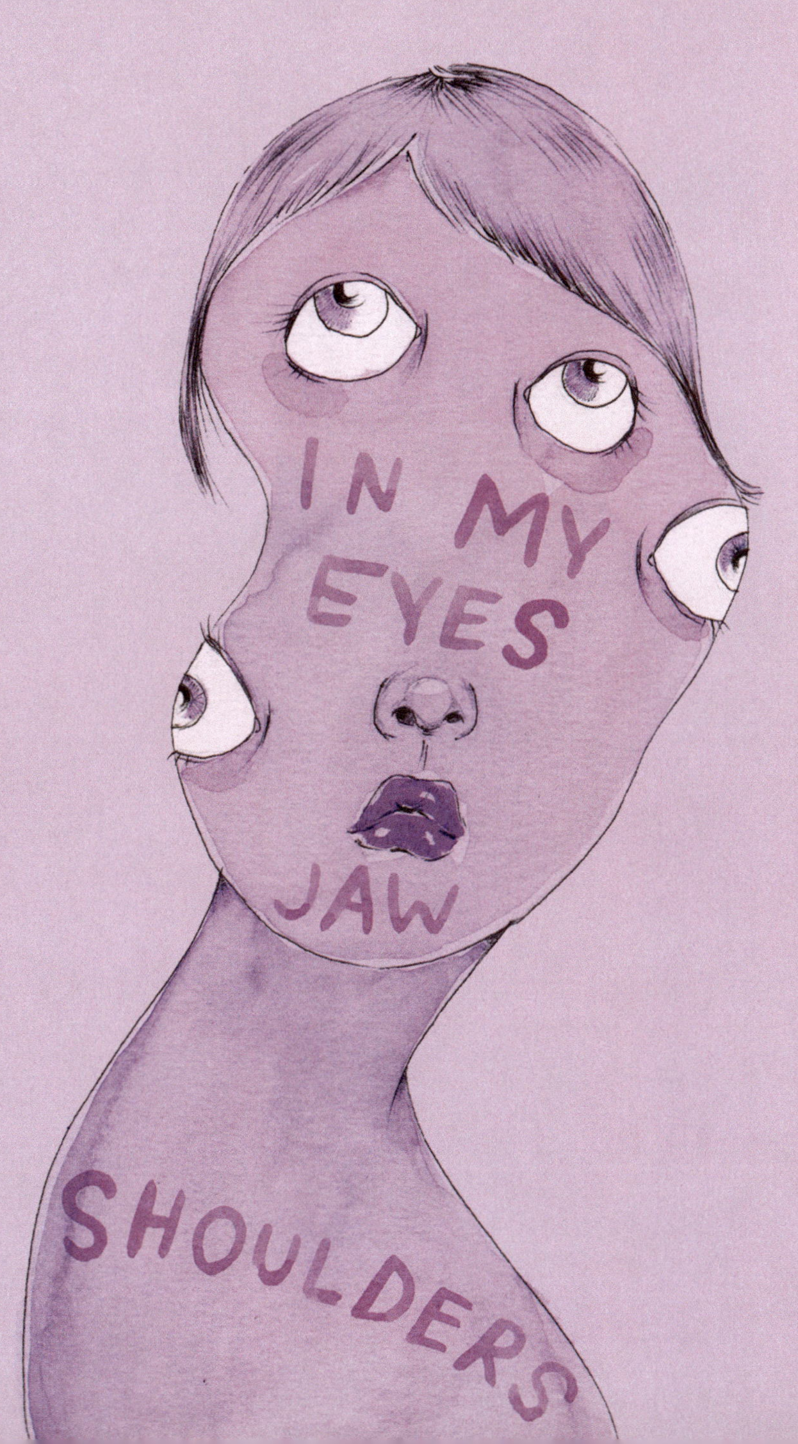
IN MY
EYES
JAW
SHOULDERS

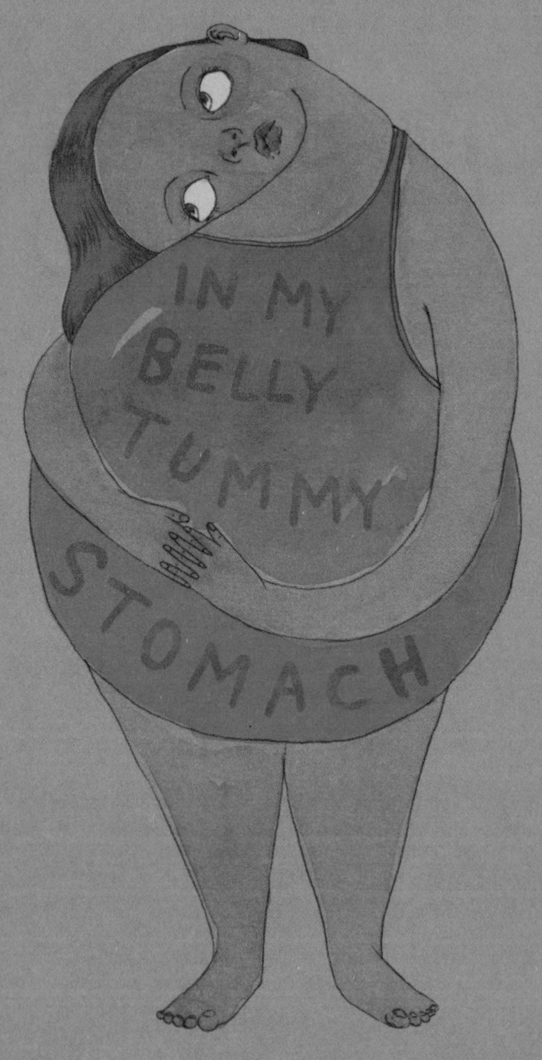
IN MY
BELLY
TUMMY
STOMACH

HAIR
TOES
IN
MY
ARMS

IN
MY
LUNGS
SOLAR
PLEXUS

IN
MY
BACK
LEGS
FEET

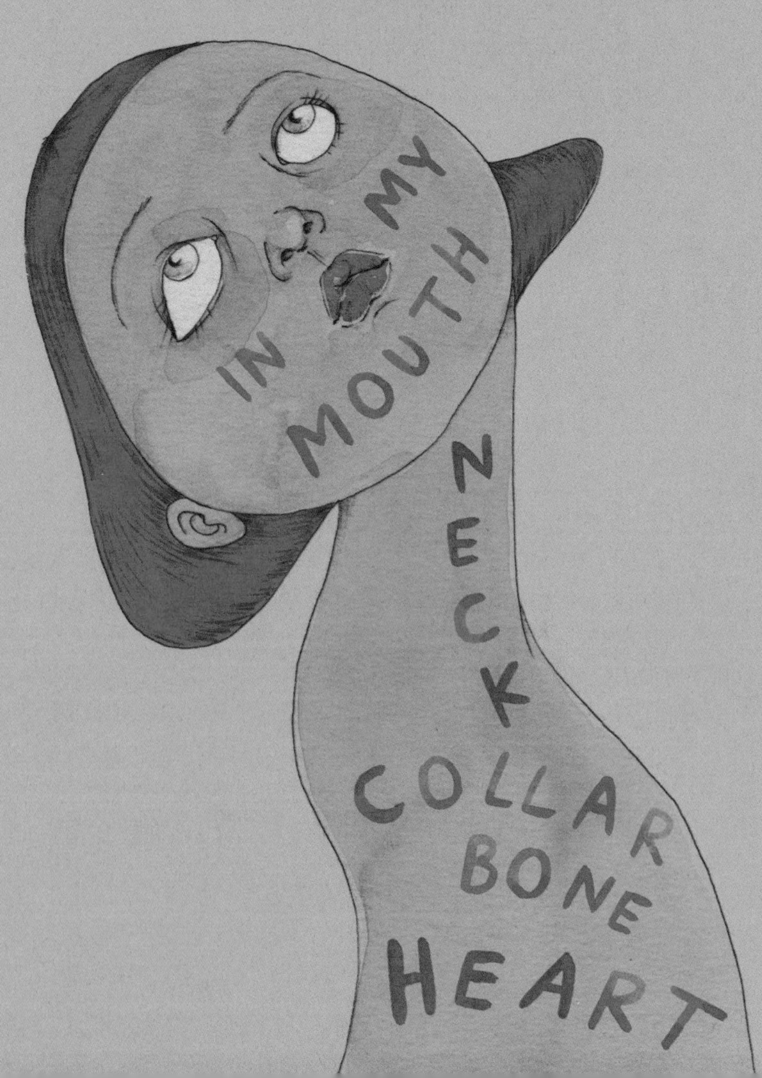
IN MY
MOUTH
NECK
COLLAR
BONE
HEART

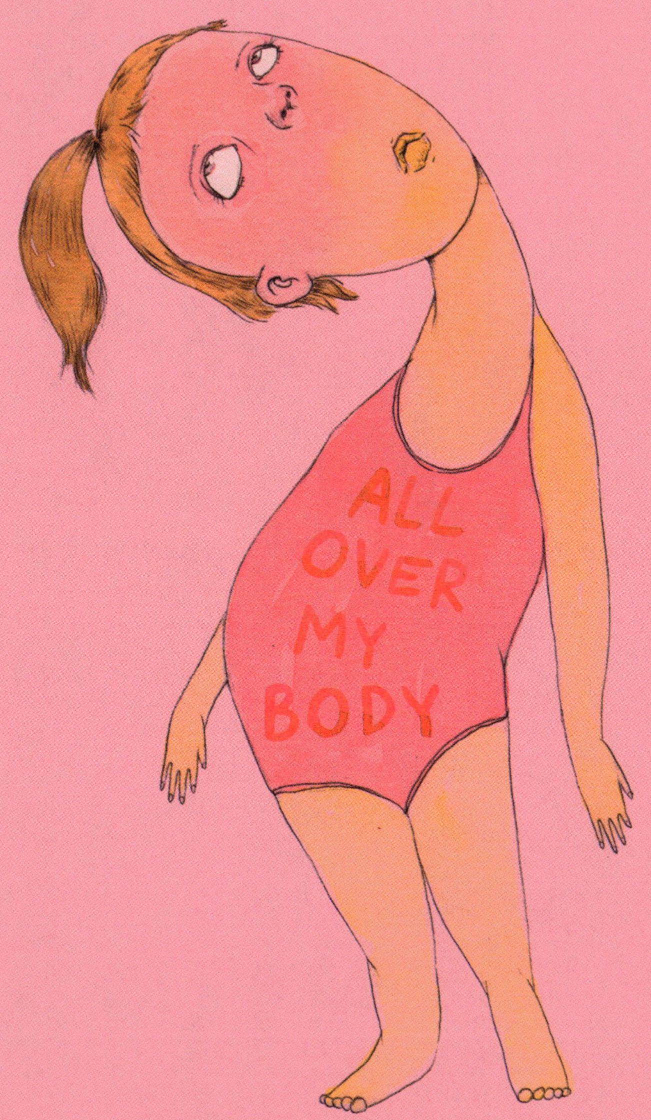
ALL
OVER
MY
BODY

AIR

3

One day, when I was home alone, a 60-foot tree fell on my house during a windstorm. I'm the only one who felt it fall. I felt the force of it, I felt the sound of the bark pressing itself into the cold earth, I felt the motion of frantic branches scraping my windows, I felt the buzz of the electrical lines as they ripped from my house, I felt the violent silence and darkness that filled the air when it was all over. I felt everything, all at once, condensed into a second or two. Everyone else saw the aftermath. They told me it must have been terrifying, but no one seemed to really understand what it was like. Seeing the aftermath and feeling something as it happens is not the same. The aftermath of destruction is not the same as being destroyed. You don't know unless you know.

When people see me on fire they only see the aftermath. The wreckage, something that needs to be tended to, cleaned up. They never see what lives under the fire.

It's strange to think that a 60-foot tree was uprooted by something as seemingly harmless as air. It's always the things you can't see or hold that cause the most devastating kind of destruction. Before the windstorm, the tree looked perfectly healthy. It was tall and leafy and never showed any sign of weakness.

But once it split apart in the wind, its vulnerabilities were out on display for all to witness. Small circles of rot in the middle of its core, branches that stretched out too far without properly anchoring themselves to the trunk that desperately wanted to hold them. It was easy to see everything in the aftermath, but before the fall even an expert arborist could not have predicted that a little wind could take this tree down.

I wish there was a way to see what lies under the surface of things. I used to think that maybe an X-ray or an ultrasound could give me a better idea of where the fire comes from, but no doctor has ever been able to provide me with a conclusive answer. Most of them pretend not to see the fire on my skin, instead of just admitting that they can't explain it. "It must be all in your head," they say as they rub their burnt fingers. Sometimes I look directly at the flames and try to get an answer from them myself: "What are you doing here?" I ask over and over again, but the flames just keep burning on my skin, unbothered by my incessant questioning.

this
thought
clings to me
like gum in
my hair

I LIKE SITTING
IN MY
FEELINGS AND
CALLING IT
VULNERABILITY

BUT BY DEFINITION I DON'T WANT TO BE

"SUSCEPTIBLE TO PHYSICAL OR EMOTIONAL ATTACK OR HARM"

I JUST WANT TO
FALL IN LOVE
WITH THE
UNCURATED
VERSION
OF THINGS

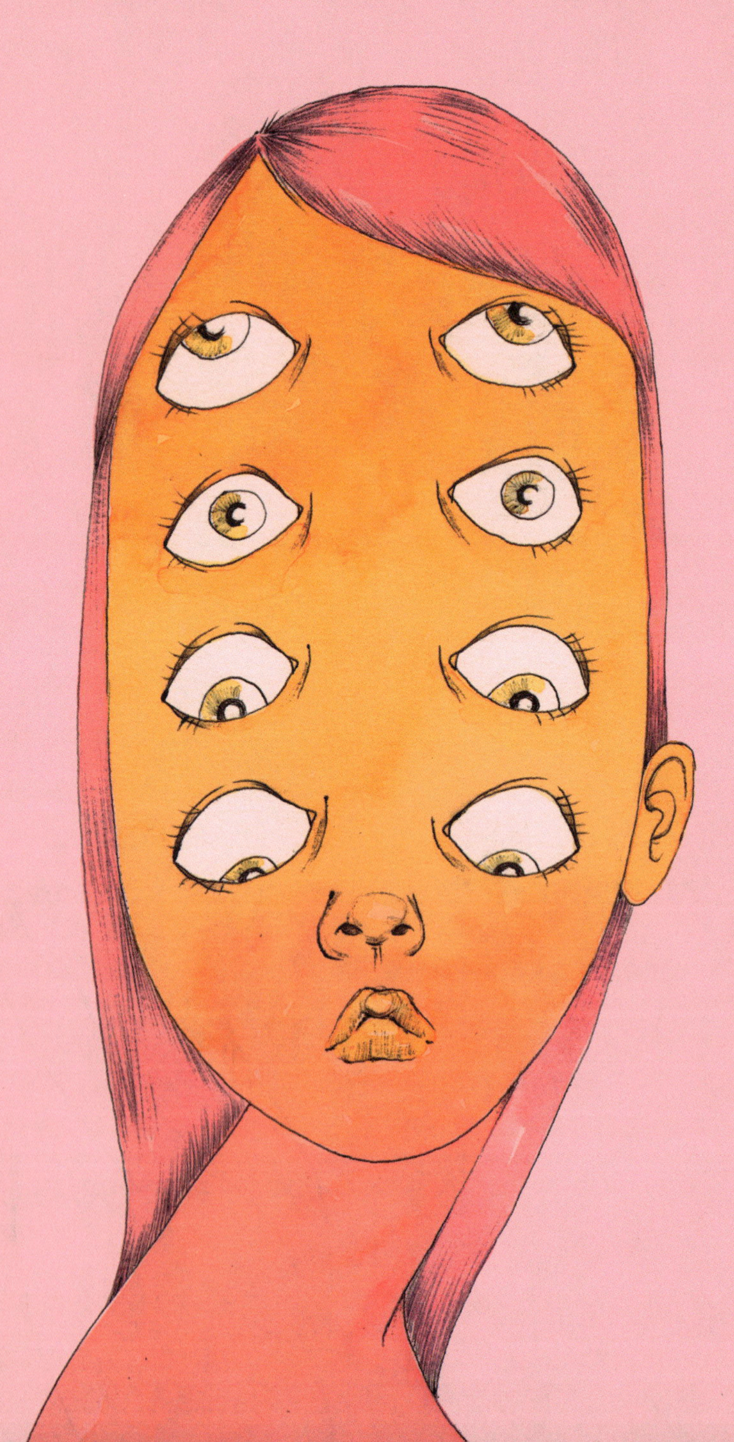

Distraction
In small
Increments
For hours
And hours
And hours
And hours
Loneliness
Never felt so
Overwhelming

I don't want to look at
The big picture
Anymore
I just want to
Collect
Small
Sad
Feelings
And call it
Hope

I packed my sadness
And moved
Somewhere beautiful
My pain didn't change
But at least now
I can pretend
It looks quite pretty

EARTH

4

When you've been on fire long enough, eventually, all people see are flames. Everything you say is tainted by fire. "It must be the fire talking," they say, as they ignore and overrule opinions that would have been taken seriously if only you had been able to hide the fact that you were a person who burns sometimes.

My dad is a volcano. Fire has lived inside of him his entire life, always close to the surface, always ready to erupt. I sometimes wonder if I caught my flames from him, if his volatile way of managing his own affliction left its mark on me. Our fires are similar but we tame them differently. I'm always fighting my fire, never letting it win, never letting it become who I am. I'm not a fire, I'm just a girl who catches fire. My dad let his heat eat him alive, he became a volcano, the explosive centre of a perimeter of destruction. He can't separate himself from it or disavow it, so he tries to validate it and convince the world that volcanoes are as peaceful as mountains.

Our differing fire management techniques make it difficult for us to get along. I think he needs to see his fire in me, to make it less lethal by relabeling it as inheritance instead of pain.

No matter how hard I fight the fire off, I can't seem to get rid of it completely. Some things take root even if you don't plant them or tend to them. There is so much that grows in the dark under the earth, under my skin, feelings buried deep. The roots of feelings not yet ready to reveal themselves. Sometimes roots give you life, sometimes they hold you back. Sometimes you stop growing because your roots are tangled in resentment. Sometimes growing up means growing out of the soil that once fed you.

there's a heaping
pile of pain
hiding under
all this rage

You love me like a thief:
You tell me I'm everything
You take everything from me

I tried to fit
My big feelings
Into polite
Little smiles
But every piece
Set aside as excess
Just grew back
As anxiety

I was drawn to you
Because we could be
Our most miserable
Selves
Together

For a while
It was nice
To feel anger
As a team

But in the company
Of our misery
I became the ghost
To your vampire
A passive audience
For you to feed

Maybe I knew
What I was
Getting myself
Into
Maybe I thought
I could
Be
Both loved
And angry

You live under my feelings
Splitting everything in two:

1. How I feel

2. How I feel
because of you

OTHER FEELINGS

5

I spent the entire day holding myself together, following the seams of my self-control with my fingers, trying to press the stitches down before they unravel. I could taste the fire on my tongue, but I resisted it. I resisted it when I woke up by getting out of bed. I resisted it on the bus to work by getting off at the right stop. I resisted it at work by smiling politely at all of my coworkers. I pressed my smile against my teeth, pushing my cheeks out to my ears, pressing my tongue against the roof of my mouth. I extended my face so forcefully that I managed to successfully stop any other emotion from making a visible appearance.

The workday is over now and I'm too frenetic to wait for a bus and too poor to call a taxi, so I am walking home instead. I thought walking would keep my mind distracted from my body, which has been smoking silently all day. I'm reminded of that small American town on fire, burning from the inside, dying in slow breaths.

I'm about halfway home now and I'm starting to give up. My smile is slipping off my face like eye makeup after a good cry. Walking is not helping. I can feel tiny sparks slipping through my fingers, leaving a singed trail behind me. I think there is someone following me now, picking up the pieces. I try to walk faster, but they walk faster too.

I start to run, but there are flames falling out of me every time my feet hit the ground. The more I try to escape my fire, the more fires I set. The flames light a path for this person behind me who is running now too.

I turn quickly into a small group of trees and end up in a park in the centre of the city. My body is feeling tired and I know I will need to stop soon. I see a bench behind a few trees and run towards it. I think I hear footsteps behind me but I don't look back.

I'm sitting on the bench now. There is a man-made pond in front of me, overflowing with greenish water and adorned with a fountain that creates a contrived current. It's funny how cities try to recreate nature but in a more controlled kind of way. It never looks as good. City nature is like the fake smile of nature. A tree molded into a sidewalk, a patch of grass in the middle of a busy street, a fake pond in front of me. Everyone knows it's not supposed to be there, but we accept it obediently.

I know it's a matter of seconds now. I can feel the fire, angered by how forcefully I held it back all day. I thought I was taming the flames, but maybe I was just delaying them, while they folded in on themselves, growing in strength, pushing up against my skin, biding their time. My face is starting to crackle, and my fingers and my legs and my toes are starting to ignite. The fire doesn't usually take hold of my whole body this way. It usually takes over small parts of me, leaving me with enough will to pull myself back out of the flames. But I held this fire back for too long and it has decided to retaliate. I'm fully on fire now, my whole body is held hostage by the flames. I can feel the bench beneath me start to burn: the boards getting warm under my fingers, the smell of burning wood in the air. The fire is escaping me now, spreading to everything, the water of the pond, the wind dancing through my hair, the ground holding up my feet, flames upon flames, things that aren't supposed to burn are now on fire.

I don't know what to do. Surely someone will see me soon. A girl on fire on a bench in front of a fake pond in the middle of a city park. What if I set the whole city on fire, what if my flames cause people harm, what if everything bad that happens next is because of me and my inability to stop myself from catching fire? I'm having a hard time seeing now, everything is red and orange and a little bit blue. Maybe this is it for me, this is who I was always supposed to be.

There is something in the distance coming towards me now. A figure, getting closer. Their hands are full of sparks and flames, collected behind me while I ran from them. I want to warn them to stay away, to tell them that they too will catch fire if they come too close. But when I open my mouth the only thing that comes out is flames. The person is in front of me now, close enough that I can see how familiar they look, even though I know for sure that I have never seen them before.

To my surprise, they seem completely unfazed by the fire and keep moving closer. They put their hand on my shoulder and whisper in my ear, "I know how you feel." And in that moment my fire comes back to me, letting go of everything else, it's contained on my skin again, still here but in a more familiar and manageable way. The stranger sits down next to me now and starts catching fire a little too. They take my hand and we stare at the pond as our flames run their course.

Other people are joining us now, one by one they sit and stand near us, and slowly break out into flames. I feel the fire all around me now. The sun is setting but the charred space around us holds onto the warmth and the light.

I don't know how long I will stay here or if I'll ever stop burning, but for now, it's nice to have a place to burn together.

can we stand in
for him
together
stand up
for each other
can we praise
where he always criticized

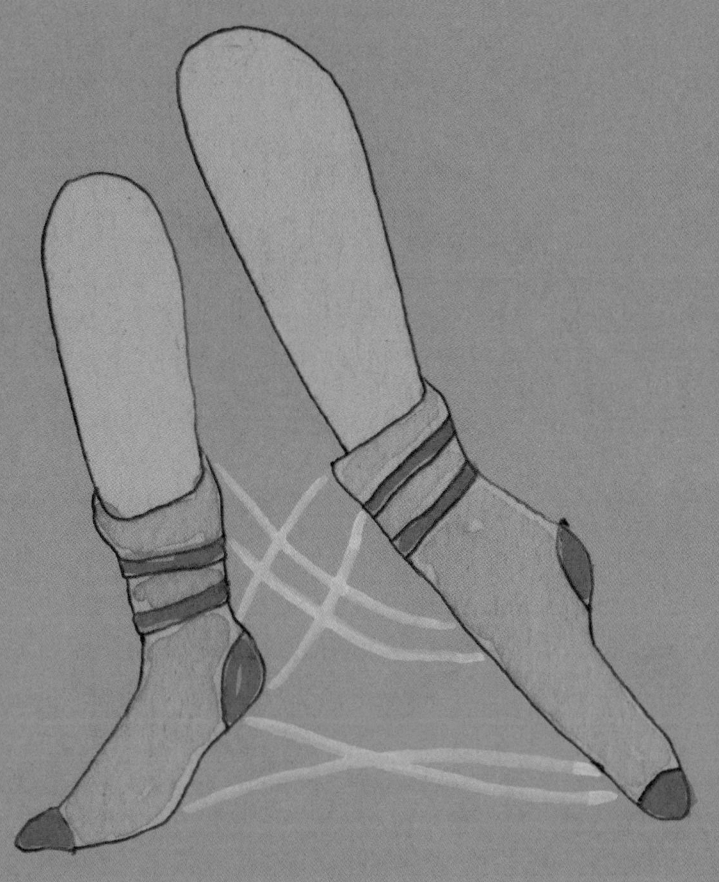

can we stitch
our disappointment
together
hold it
together
watch it run
like stockings
together

can we take
each other
out for ice cream
every year on our birthday
we'll always remember
when he does not

can we stand in
for him
together
for each other
can we give him back his name
can we become
all the things
he warned us about

and never brush it off
or fake a smile
or tell each other
to stop crying

I ALWAYS
CARRY
EVERYTHING
WITH ME

HELLO

Ambivalently Yours is a semi-anonymous, aggressively sensitive, perpetually ambivalent, Canadian visual artist, animator and writer. Her work aims to highlight the transformative potential that exists within conflicting emotions. Her art has been exhibited locally and internationally, shared virally on the Internet, and featured prominently in online media publications, teenage blogs, and zines worldwide.

ambivalentlyyours.com

IG / FB / TT: @ambivalentlyyours
TW: @ambivalentlyyou

THOUGHT
CATALOG
Books

Thought Catalog Books is a publishing imprint of Thought Catalog, a digital magazine for thoughtful storytelling, and is owned and operated by The Thought & Expression Company, an independent media group based in Brooklyn, NY. Founded in 2010, we are committed to helping people become better communicators and listeners to engender a more exciting, attentive, and imaginative world. As a publisher and media platform, we help creatives all over the world realize their artistic vision and share it in print and digital forms with audiences across the globe.

ThoughtCatalog.com | **Thoughtful Storytelling**

ShopCatalog.com | **Shop Books + Curated Products**

MORE FROM THOUGHT CATALOG BOOKS

How to Laugh in Ironic Amusement During Your Existential Crisis
—James McCrae

Ceremony
—Brianna Wiest

Don't F*cking Panic
—Kelsey Darragh

The Magic Within
—Danica Gim

THOUGHT
CATALOG
Books

THOUGHTCATALOG.COM
NEW YORK · LOS ANGELES